Bernkastel-Kues, Moselle, Germany.

This tour encompasses five cities, four countries, and two world wars. The tour visits one of the most beautiful sections of river in Europe, a Roman capital, a national park where wild cats roam free and a town where Christmas gifts are sold all year. It will take you from the highest point in the Netherlands to below the streets of Arras.

This tour can be completed in any month. Bruges and Valkenburg can be enjoyed the year round and both have large Christmas markets. The Moselle valley comes alive with wine festivals in the autumn. The Eifel National Park will be delightful from spring to autumn. Visiting the First World War cemeteries is a moving experience at any time of year, and perhaps more so during the 100th anniversary period. The theatre of war is now an attractive and fertile agricultural landscape, but in some respects the best time to visit is on bitterly cold, windy or rainy days when you can get a better sense of the suffering endured.

Distances have been provided between each destination, but no time limit has been specified. It is for you to take as much time as you need. That said, this tour could be completed in a week if only one night was spent in each place, but two weeks should be sufficient.

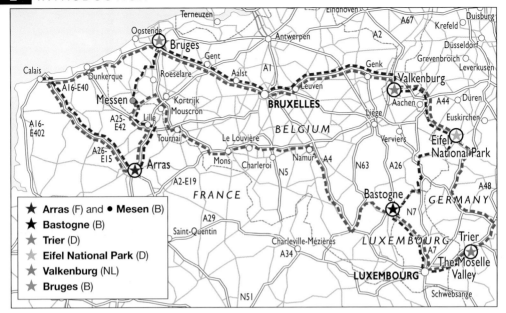

This tour can be followed as a circlular or a linear tour from France to Germany. The circular tour is marked in blue on the map above, while the linear tour is marked in pink. The entries in this book follow the circular tour, but at the end of each section the subsequent page number is provided for those following the linear tour.

Linear tour highlighted pink on the map above: 850km, 9hrs driving.
(See dotted pink line on map above)
Calais (F) – **Arras** (F), 108km, 1hr 9mins.
Arras (F) – **Ieper** (B), 90km, 1hr 10mins.
Ieper (B) – **Bruges** (B), 73.2km, 1hr.
Bruges (B) – **Valkenburg** (NL), 236km, 2hrs 20mins.
Valkenburg (NL) – **Eifel National Park** (D) 74.9km, 1hr 12mins.
Eifel National Park (D) – **Bastogne** (B) – 150km, 2hrs.
Bastogne (B) – **Trier** (D) – 137km, 1hr 20mins.

Circular tour highlighted blue on the map above: 1183km, 13hrs driving.
(See dotted blue line on map above)
Calais (F) – **Arras** (F), 108km, 1hr 9mins.
Arras (F) – **Ieper** (B), 90km, 1hr 10mins.
Ieper (B) – **Bastogne** (B), 270km, 2hrs 30mins.
Bastogne (B) – **Trier** (D), 137km, 1hr 20mins.
Trier (D) – **Eifel National Park** (D) 115km, 1hr 30mins.
Eifel National Park (D) – **Valkenburg** (NL), 75.4km, 1hr 10mins.
Valkenburg (NL) – **Bruges** (B) 236km, 2hrs 20mins.
Bruges (B) – **Calais** (F) 115km, 1hr 14mins.

Faubourg-d'Amiens WWI Commonwealth Cemetery near Arras, France.

How to use this guide

Green text boxes highlight driving directions.

Walking directions are highlighted in a pink text box with a walking symbol 🚶.

Each tourist attraction is identifed by number or letter on the supporting map and text.

Each attraction has GPS coordinates for use with in-vehicle or handheld navigators.

Supporting information, such as where to park, stay, eat and other useful information, is found in a column on the side of the relevant page.

For further information on motorhome stopovers purchase All the Aires France or All the Aires Belgium, Holland and Luxembourg from www.VicariousBooks.co.uk

Key to Symbols

🚐	Motorhome Stopover
🏕	Camping
🏨	Hotel
✕	Restaurant/Café
🛒	Shop
🅿	Parking
☆	Tips and Tricks
🛈	Further information
🪖	Additional places to visit
✼	Festivals
🚶	Walks
WC	Toilets

Guide to prices

🚐 Stopovers	€ = €1-€5	€€ = €5-€13	€€€ = €13-€20	€€€€ = €20+
🏕 Campsites	€ = €1-€15	€€ = €15-€30	€€€ = €30+	
🏨 Hotels	€ = €1-€50	€€ = €100	€€€ = €100-€150	€€€€ = €150+
✕ Restaurants	€ = €1-€25pp	€€ = €25-€50pp	€€€ = €50-€75pp	€€€€ = €75pp+
	🏕 = FREE			

WWI cemeteries and Arras

Ablain-Saint-Nazaire

Above and right Notre Dame de Lorette National Cemetery.

★ WWI: The battle for Arras and Vimy Ridge

The Central Powers of Germany and Hungary-Austria invaded this area of France in 1914. The area was defended throughout the war by forces from France and the Commonwealth, mainly British, based at Arras, New Zealanders and Australians, who mined the tunnels under Arras, and Canadians, who stormed the ridge in 1917. This section of the tour takes in the high and low points of the battlefield.

> *From Calais head south on the A26 towards Paris. North of Arras exit the A26 at Junction 6.1, sp 'Noeux les Mines', then follow sp 'Noeux les Mines' onto the D937. Just before Souchez turn right onto the D58E3, sp 'N.D. de Lorette'. Drive uphill to the* **Cimetière National (1)**, *a WWI French cemetery and memorial. There is a large level parking area outside the gates and a viewing platform opposite.*

(1) Notre Dame de Lorette Cimetière National
N50°24.003' E002°43.149'
Free entry; Open daily.

Before you enter the cemetery walk across to the viewing platform located opposite the main entrance. Look across the contested coalfield to Vimy Ridge, the high ground in the distance. Historic slag heaps are also visible to the left. Following the initial invasion, it took French soldiers 12 months to regain Lorette Hill, where you are standing. Crucially, the Germans still had control of the coalfields and factories below. Commonwealth forces took over Lorette Hill in March 1916 and it is from here that Canadian soldiers advanced towards Vimy Ridge on the 9th of April 1917.

The Cimetière National de Notre-Dame is the largest French war cemetery. 40,000 soldiers are laid to rest here, regrettably 22,000 are unknown. The soldiers' religious faiths are identified by headstone shape or by symbolic carvings. A few plain headstones mark atheist graves. The white stone basilica acts as a beacon during daylight hours and the adjacent tower houses a lantern that is illuminated nightly. Since 1920 visitors have been welcomed by a Voluntary Guard of Honor who also rekindle the Eternal Flame every Sunday.

> *Drive back to the D937 and continue south for 2.5km toward Arras. Pass through Souchez and* **Cabaret-Rouge British Cemetery (2)** *is 700m on the right.*

Cabaret-Rouge British WWI Cemetery near Arras.

Arras

www.arras.fr

Park

🚐 Rue des Rosati　　　🕱
N50°17.688' E002°47.310'

🅿 P2 Mail des Rosati　　🕱
N50°17.714' E002°47.121'

Eat

Light bites are available from bakeries and cafés around the two squares.

✗ Between Terre et Mer　€
N50°17.466' E002°46.745'
12 Rue de la Taillerie
www.betweenterreetmer.fr

✗ Le Petit rat Porteur　€€
N50°17.471' E002°46.741'
11 Rue de la Taillerie
www.lepetitratporteur.fr

Historic slag heaps.

(2) Cabaret-Rouge British Cemetery
N50°22.839' E002°44.494'
Free entry; Open daily.

During the war commonwealth cemeteries took on local names and these have been kept to the current day. Cabaret-Rouge was a local café until it was destroyed by artillery shells in March 1915. Its name was also used to identify the local sector and a communication trench that led troops up to the frontline.

Post war repatriation of fallen commonwealth soldiers was an impossible task and the decision was made by The Commonwealth War Graves Commission (CWGC) to bury the dead as close as possible to their place of death. Many bodies were moved from the surroundings into the landscaped places of rest you can see today.

CWGC cemeteries normally have a low perimeter wall, are meticulously maintained and there are often flowers planted in front of the headstones. Although no two cemeteries are the same, there are several features to look for. For example, cemeteries with 40 graves or more have a Cross of Sacrifice, and cemeteries with over 1,000 burials have a Stone of Remembrance.

Cabaret-Rouge British Cemetery has 7,655 graves, having taken in bodies from over 100 other local cemeteries. Soldiers from all over the commonwealth rested here until the millennium when one unknown Canadian soldier was taken home in an act of remembrance for the 116,000 Canadian soldiers who lost their lives during the war. A headstone in Plot 8, Row E, Grave 7 marks his original resting place. You will pass many cemeteries on this journey, all of which preserve the memory not only of the fallen but also of the local sacrifices made.

> *Continue towards Arras on the D937. In 4km turn left into the small parking area for **Neuville St Vaast German War Cemetery (3)**. The parking area is big enough for three coaches and is easy to drive past, but is signed. Toilets are adjacent to the entrance.*

Cross of Sacrifice

Stone of Rememberance

Above Neuville St Vaast German WWI Cemetery near Arras. **Right** Cabaret Rouge British cemetery.

(3) Neuville St Vaast German War Cemetery
N50°20.598' E002°45.112'
Free entry; Open daily.

Post war consolidation has made Neuville St Vaast the biggest German cemetery in France. 44,833 German soldiers are buried here, of which 8,040 are unknown. In common with other German military cemeteries, one headstone marks more than one grave. The German War Graves Commission reorganised the cemetery during the 1970s and they planted many trees that can still be seen today. The landscape is simple and has a natural feel which reflects the German belief of returning to nature.

There is an information panel outside the cemetery and inside the gates there is a tabletop relief map carved in stone that depicts the theatre of war on Vimy Ridge.

Continue on the D937 towards Arras. Follow signs to 'St Laurent B.', then 'Parc des Expositions'. The motorhome parking is adjacent to the exhibition hall parking on Rue des Rosati, signed. There is plenty of roadside parking and a large car park sp 'P2'.

(4) Arras
Parking: N50°17.688' E002°47.310'

Arras was bombarded during WWI and eventually reduced to rubble by artillery fire from Vimy Ridge.

(A) The Grand Square
N50°17.524' E002°46.819'

The city of Arras was rebuilt post-war, but the facades of the town hall and the two main squares, the Grand' Place and the Place des Heros, were reconstructed true to the original Flemish design. Behind the facades the buildings are fabricated with reinforced concrete frames.

Shop

In the central squares there are plenty of shops to browse in. Local ginger biscuits, called Speculoos, are available from the bakeries.

An excellent range of local and imported beer is available from the beer shop which is located in the opposite corner of the square from the town hall.

Stay

Arras Stopover
N50°17.688' E002°47.310'
Rue des Rosati
10 spaces; Services €2

La Paille-Haute €€
N50°16.401' E002°56.912'
Boiry-Notre-Dame, 12km from Arras
Open Apr-Oct
www.la-paille-haute.com

Holiday Inn Express Arras €€
N50°17.211' E002°46.767'
3 rue Docteur Brassart
www.holidayinn-arras.com

Arras City

Rue du 8 Mai 1945
Avenue Winston Churchill Avenue Winston Churchill
Rue de la Croix de Grès
Rue Michelet
P P P P P
D 266   D 266   D 266
P
Quai du Riv
Rue de l'Abbé Pierre
Rue de la Fraternité
Rue Alexis Halette
Rue de l'Égalité
Boulevard Georges Besnier
Rue Baudimont
Rue Jules Ferry
Rue Roger Salengro
Rue de Turenne
Rue du Bloc
Rue Miaulers
Rue des Bouchers de Cité
Rue Pierre Bérégovoy
Rue des Teinturiers
École Paul Bert
l'uvis de Chavannes
Rue Auguste Dumand
P
Gendarmerie
Rue Dambrine
l'Hippodrome
Boulevard du Président Allende
Rue des Carabiniers d'Arras
Rue Saint-Aubert
École Séverine
Rue de la Paix
Rue des Hochettes
Rue André Gatoux
Rue d'Amiens
Rue de Paris
Rue du 29 Juillet
Rue Saint-Aubert
École primaire privée Saint-Joseph
Rue Paul
Rue Braque
D 265
Rue d'Amiens
Rue Sainte-Claire
Arras
Cours de Verdun
Rue des Grands Fours
Rue des Capucins Rue des 4 Crosses
265
Rue Georges Santerne
P

Collège Jehan Bodel
Rue de Beaufort
Bou
Rue Louis Hélie
Lycée général et technologique Robespierre
École maternelle Oscar Cléret
Rue Jeanne d'Arc
Rue Frédéric Degeorge
Rue Paul Langevin
Avenue des Fusillés
P
P
Rue Beffara
Rue Jeanne d'Arc
Jean Zay
Espace vert des autes-Fontaines
Avenue du Mémorial des Fusillés
Boulevard du Général de Gaulle
Jardin du Gouverneur
Rue Lamartine
P
Le Crinchon
Rue Adam de la Halle
Rue de Grigny
Rue d'Achicourt
Citadelle d'Arras
Rue Frédéric Degeorge
Rue Frédéric Degeorge
Cité du Polygone
Rue François Lambert
Rue Roger Salengro
Rue du

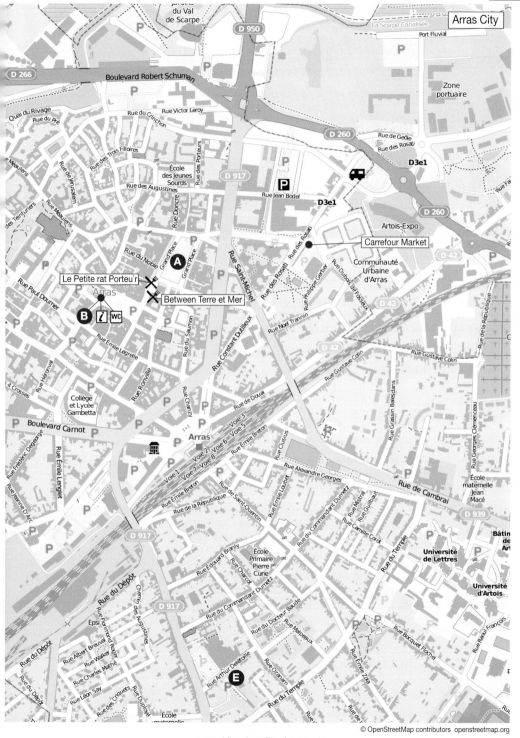

Arras City

Arras from the Hôtel de Ville belfry.

⚐ Arras town centre
Total distance: 3.2km, 1.9 miles
With your back to the Carrefour Supermarket on Rue des Rosati, cross the road and follow the footpath. In 250m cross the road at the traffic-lighted zebra crossing. Go straight on for 100m into the **Grand Square (A)**. Walk across the square into the middle. Read information on the **Grand Square (A)**.

⚐ Continue across the square and down Rue de la Taillerie. This takes you to the second smaller square and the **Hôtel de Ville (B)**.

(B) Hôtel de Ville, Belfry and Boves
N50°17.462' E002°46.630'
Open daily Jan-Apr and Sept-Dec 10am-noon and 2-6pm, May-Aug 9am-6pm. www.visitarras.com
Belfry: €2.90; Accessed via a lift and then steep steps.
Boves: €5.20; Visitors to these caves need to be agile and may be required to crouch or kneel to pass through the tunnels.
Belfry and Boves combined ticket: €6.80.

The Hôtel de Ville can be viewed from the outside, inside, above and below. The Tourist Office is located inside the town hall and they issue tickets for the belfry and caves. Take the lift to the belfry for a 360° aerial view of Arras and its surroundings. The lift shaft gives away the hidden concrete secrets.

A much bigger secret known as the *boves* is hidden below the town hall and, for that matter, all of Arras. Medieval cellars and tunnels and were extended by Commonwealth troops, mainly New Zealanders, to create an underground city in the soft chalk. Cellars became bomb shelters and tunnels housed subways, tramways and railways. The *boves* became a second town; electricity was generated, kitchens cooked, medical centres with operating theatres treated the sick and wounded and latrines took away waste.

⚐ 20 minutes' walk east from the centre there are two places of military history that are worth visiting, **(C)** and **(D)**. Both have on-street parking and they are only 300m apart.

Wellington Quarry - WWI quarries under Arras.

(C) Faubourg-d'Amiens Military Hospital Cemetery
N50°17.221' E002°45.640'
Free entry; Open daily; On-street parking available.

There was already a military cemetery on this site in 1916 when the British Army relieved the French at Arras, but it was eventually removed and only the Commonwealth cemetery now remains. At the entrance is the Arras Memorial which displays the names of nearly 35,000 British, New Zealand and South African soldiers whose bodies were never found.

(D) Vauban Citadel
N50°17.077' E002°45.785'
Free entry; Guided tours every Sunday at 3.30pm June-Sept, €6.40; On street parking available.

The citadel is a preserved star fort with UNESCO World Heritage status.

'Mur des Fusillés' is located on Avenue du Mémorial des Fusillés beside the outer citadel wall. This memorial acts as remembrance for World War II French resistance suspects who were shot by the Nazis. Plaques bearing the names and ages of those shot have been fixed to the wall: N50°16.927' E002°45.432'.

> *Before you leave Arras drive to **Wellington Quarry (E)**, following sp 'Carrière-Wellington' in Arras. There is some parking outside and additional parking at the adjacent supermarket.*

(E) Wellington Quarry
N50°16.856' E002°46.979'
€6.80; Open daily 10am-12.30pm and 1.30-6pm, except Jan 1, 27-28, June 29, Dec 25 and the three weeks after Christmas; Tours in English and French depart hourly between 10am-5pm Feb-Dec.

Festivals

✵ A Christmas market is held in the central squares from Nov 30-Dec 24.

✵ The Main Square music festival is held in the main square on either the last weekend of June or the first weekend of July. Entry €49, or weekend pass for €115. www.mainsquarefestival.fr

WWI commemorative dates
25 April ANZAC day (Australia and New Zealand)
4 Nov (Italy)
11 Nov Armistice Day (Commonwealth countries, France and Belgium)
Volkstrauertag falls in the middle of Nov (Germany)

WWI commemorative flowers
Poppy – Commonwealth countries
Cornflour – France and Belgium
Forget-me-not – Germany

Above and right Canadian National Vimy Memorial and WWI trenches near Arras.

The tour starts in a lift down to the tunnels and chambers. Next there is a 50 minute level walk around the mine on a wooden walkway which is occasionally wet. There are no handrails or seats in the quarry. The final element is a 10 minute video. www.carriere-wellington.com, www.arras.fr/tourisme

Travel back in time to the 9th of April 1917. Eight days before the battle of Arras 24,000 Allied troops had amassed right under the Germans' noses, and feet. Housing all those soldiers took months of preparation. Miners from all over the Commonwealth dug and adapted tunnels that dated back to medieval times.

Under the St Sauveur area of town British and Scottish troops gave the tunnels names like Glasgow and Manchester, but New Zealand miners prepared and named Wellington Quarry and nine other areas. Inside the tunnels there are plenty of reminders which help you to understand how the Allied soldiers lived and prepared for the Battle of Arras.

Exit Arras to the north on the D55 and follow signs to 'Parc et Memorial Canadien' (5). Turn right into Vimy interpretation centre. Parking onsite.

(5) Parc et Memorial Canadien
N50°22.355' E002°46.136'
Free entrance; Open daily 10am-5pm Feb-Nov.

Vimy Ridge is one of the few places in France where the battlefield is preserved as it was at the end of WWI. Grass and trees now cover the churned mud, but the bunkers, bomb holes and restored trenches help to build a picture of the extent and complexity of the battlefield. You are welcome to walk through preserved trenches and look out of the machine gun turrets towards the enemy lines just further than a grenade throw away. We recommend that you join one of the free 50-minute tours bookable at the visitor centre. You will be led by young Canadians who will take you through the tunnels and passionately explain the history.

*From the interpretation centre drive or walk 800m to the **Canadian National Vimy Memorial (6)**. Onsite parking is located opposite the small Moroccan division war memorial.*

Mur des Fusillés, UNESCO Citadel Star fort, Arras.

(6) Canadian National Vimy Memorial
N50°22.752' E002°46.203'
Free entry; Open daily.

The Battle of Vimy Ridge was the first time that all four divisions of the Canadian Expeditionary Force battled together as one. Their achievements and sacrifices at Vimy and at other theatres during WWI are now remembered here. The impressive Canadian Memorial stands tall at the end of the ridge from which point you can see the strategic advantage gained by controlling this area of high ground. Look back across the coal slag heaps and Lens town to Notre Dame de Lorette Cimetière National on top of the hill. Carved into the stone monument are the names of 11,285 Canadian soldiers who died in France but whose final resting place was unknown.

> *From Vimy head to Ploegsteert. First drive to Lens. From Lens follow the N41 towards Lille. Turn left onto the A25 towards Bailleul. Exit the A25 at Junction 8 and go straight over the roundabout onto the D945, sp 'Armentieres'. Follow the D945 for 5km then turn left at the roundabout onto the D7, sp 'Ploegsteert'. In 500m cross the Belgian border and the D7 becomes the N58. Follow the N58 for 4.5km then exit, sp 'Ploegsteert'. At the stop junction turn left, sp 'Ploegsteert', and follow the road for 4km. In **Ploegsteert (7)** park at the Mairie, which is next to the church, adjacent to the N365 roundabout in the centre of town: N50°43.579' E002°52.816'.*

WWI in Flanders: Churchill and Hitler

By coincidence, Winston Churchill and Adolf Hitler were possibly in the same place at the same time during WWI. Churchill, a Lieutenant-Colonel, was the Commanding Officer of the 6th Battalion of the Royal Scots Fusiliers at Ploegsteert from January to May 1916 and Hitler served as a dispatch runner all along the western front throughout the war. During WWII Adolf Hilter returned to Messines and visited Notre Dame de Lorette Cimetière National.

(7) Ploegsteert
N50°43.579' E002°52.816'

A memorial plaque, attached to the Mairie building, commemorates the time Winston Churchill spent in Ploegsteert.

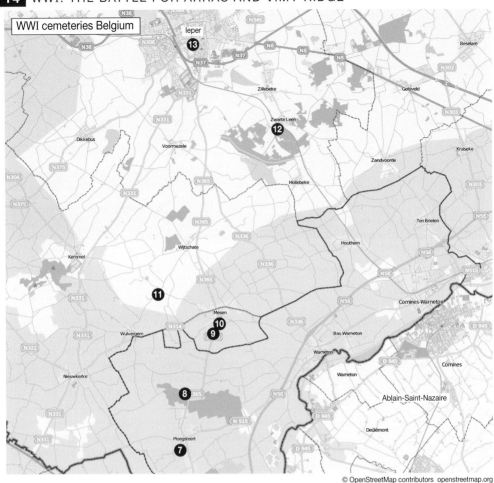

© OpenStreetMap contributors openstreetmap.org

The Belgian village of Ploegsteert was known as Plugstreet by the British soldiers who served there during WWI. This stretch of frontline was under British control for most of the war. You can be forgiven for not remembering what happened here because no set-piece battles took place.

> *Exit Ploegsteert on the N365 heading north towards Mesen. After 1.3km there are cemeteries on both sides of the road (8). There two parking bays in front of the lions.*

(8) Hyde Park Corner
N50°44.259' E002°52.938'
Free entry; Open daily.

Hyde Park Corner Cemetery is on the right and the Royal Berks Cemetery Extension is on the left and is guarded by two impressive lions. Both cemeteries were started by the Royal Berkshire Regiment. In 1930 the Royal Berks Cemetery Extension was extended from one to three plots. Plots two and three contain the exhumed bodies from the Rosenberg Château Military Cemetery and Extension Cemetery that were both located 1km northwest. The circular structure is the Ploegsteert Memorial for over 11,000 men who died in this sector during WWI but have no known grave. Their names are listed by regiment. Some of the missing have since been found in local fields, and have been buried in local cemeteries. Grave 1A located in Hyde Park Corner Cemetery marks Rifleman Samuel McBride who was executed for desertion in 1916.

There is a lot of history to discover, but there is one story that perhaps will never be forgotten. Christmas Eve 1914 was the first cold and snowy day of the war. German spirits were high and they sang carols both in German and English. Somehow a Christmas day truce was negotiated here and the same happened at numerous stretches along the western front. Soldiers met in no man's land and presents were swapped. For practical reasons the opportunity was taken to bury the fallen. Once all the necessities were done, the soldiers on both sides met and it is said that a game of football was played, but there is no historic record of the number of goals scored. A small wooden cross and information panel now marks the location of the game and explains the truce. The film *Joyeux Noel* dramatises the events. As it is not practical to drive here, see the walk below.

⚲ The Christmas Truce and Prowse Point Cemetery
Total distance 2.37km, 1.5 miles.
From Hyde Park Corner walk for 200m along the N365 towards Mesen. Turn right onto Chemin du Mont de la Hutte and take the left-hand fork. Both tracks exclude vehicles. Follow this track straight on for 1.1km to Mud Corner Cemetery on the left. Continue along the track for 270m and turn right at the end of the road. Walk 150m to the **small wooden cross memorial (F)** *on the left. Retrace your steps and instead of turning left back to Mud Corner go straight on for 100m to* **Prowse Point Cemetery (G)** *on the left. To complete the walk, continue down the track for 650m until you reach the N365. Turn left and walk 850m back to Hyde Park Corner.*

(F) The Christmas Truce
N50°44.667' E002°54.145'
Free entry; Open daily.

This commemorative cross marks the Christmas Truce of 1914 and was erected in 1999 by the Khaki Chums, a British group who in 1999 recreated the trenches and lived in them over Christmas.

(G) Prowse Point Cemetery
N50°44.657' E002°53.945'
Free entry; Open daily.

The cemetery is laid at the site of the stand by the 1st Battalion Somerset Light Infantry and 1st Battalion Hampshire Regiment in October 1914 and is named for the heroism of Major Charles Prowse, later Brigadier-General C.B. Prowse, DSO of the Somerset Light Infantry. The pond before the graves marks part

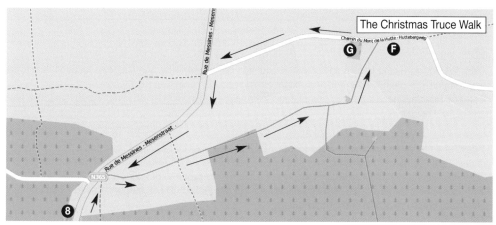

© OpenStreetMap contributors openstreetmap.org

Island of Ireland Peace Park, Mesen. © City of Mesen.

of the frontline. Besides 225 Commonwealth graves, there are also 12 German graves within the cemetery. Mesen Church can be seen on a ridge in the distance.

> *From Hyde Park Corner continue driving on the N365 towards Mesen for 2.8km. Park adjacent to the tall round tower.*

(9) Island of Ireland Peace Park
N50°45.591' E002°53.740'
Free entry; Open daily.

The Island of Ireland Peace Park opened in 1998 as a memorial to all Irish soldiers who served in WWI. The location was chosen because it is one of the few places where Irishmen fought side by side regardless of religion. The 34m high tower is built from salvaged Irish stone in the style of a traditional Irish round tower. The function of these towers is unknown, but they are normally located near to a church. There is a Peace Pledge within the centre circle of the park commemorating the fight against a common enemy. Nine stone tablets contain extracts of letters and poems written by Irish soldiers.

> *Continue 300m along the N365 into Mesen. Park at the church.*

(10) Mesen
Parking and town centre: N50°45.830' E002°53.888'

During WWI Mesen was known as Messines and was considered a strong strategic location due to its height above the plain below and the extensive system of cellars under the convent known as the Institution Royale. The village was completely destroyed by four years of shelling and fighting, but was rebuilt after the war.

Messines ridge was a natural stronghold occupied by the Germans. Following 18 months of mining and 17 days of artillery bombardment, Allied forces attacked Messines on the 7th of June 1917. The battle was famously started by detonating 600 tons of explosives hidden in 25 underground mines located under German positions. 19 mines actually exploded on the day and one exploded on the 17th of June 1955 killing a cow. Four mines on the southern flank were not detonated. The average crater size was 200 feet across and some are now pleasant farm ponds.

The Germans discovered the mine under La Petit Douve Farm by digging their own reconnaissance tunnels. They set off a bomb in their own tunnel causing the British tunnel to collapse and flood and to this day 20,000 pounds of explosives lay dormant.

Although Allied troops fought all over the ridge, it was New Zealand soldiers that took the village having advanced uphill on the now named Rue des Neo-Zélandais. The New Zealand Memorial Park stands near the top of the road.

(H) Mesen Church
N50°45.830' E002°53.888'

During the war the church was used by the Germans as a field hospital. The only part of the building to survive the war was the medieval crypt. Everything seen above ground today was built post-war. Outside a plaque explains that Adolf Hitler was treated there. Try to spend a few hours near the church so that you can listen to the carillon with 50 bells. The carillon is a series of clocks that plays a different tune every 15 minutes, including war songs, hymns and folk music. The bells are silenced at night.

Mesen
N50°45.830' E002°53.888'
www.mesen.be

Eat
✗ Mesen is the smallest city in Belgium and has a couple of bars/cafés and a Frituur (chippy) in the centre

Stay
🚐 Mesen Stopover   ✗
N50°45.830' E002°53.888'
Kerkstraat 10
2 spaces
No services

🏛 Peace Village Hostel   €
N50°45.946' E002°53.627'
Nieuwkerkestraat 9a
www.peacevillage.be

© OpenStreetMap contributors openstreetmap.org

Mesen church.

(I) New Zealand Memorial
N50°45.646' E002°53.459'
Free entry; Open daily.

250m from the parking is the New Zealand Memorial. From the memorial you can look across the ridge over the battlefield.

(K) Messines Ridge British Cemetery
N50°45.921' E002°53.452'
Free entry; Open daily.

750m from the parking is the Messines Ridge British Cemetery. This cemetery stands in the grounds of the former Institution Royale and was created after the Armistice. Graves were moved here from the battlefield around Messines and several small surrounding burial grounds.

It is possible to catch a bus from Mesen to Ieper.

> *Exit Mesen on the N314, sp 'Wolvergent'. Turn right opposite Messines Ridge British Cemetery on left. Follow this road for 2.4km and the **Pool of Peace (11)** is on the right surrounded by trees, opposite the Lone Tree Cemetery, but it is not signed. There are two parking spaces outside the Pool of Peace.*

(11) Pool of Peace
N50°46.538' E002°51.678'
Free entry; Open access.

This pool was created on the 7th of June 1917, as explained on page 16. The crater was named the Pool of Peace after the war. There is an information panel outside and steps down to the crater. On the opposite side of the road to the pool along a concrete path is Lone Tree Commonwealth Cemetery.

> *Continue straight on from the Pool of Peace. At the end of the road turn right to Wijtschate. In Wijtschate follow sp 'Ieper' onto the N365. In 5.5km turn right just after a level crossing, sp 'Hollebeke'. Follow the road for 3.5km then turn left into a 5.5t restricted road, sp 'Hill 60'. Park on the right in 300m by the memorial. The entrance to **Hill 60 (12)** is 10m away.*

(12) Hill 60
N50°49.446 E002°55.682'
Free entry; Open access.

This is another 7th of June 1916 explosion site. Hill 60 and the adjacent hill known as The Caterpillar, were areas of contention throughout WWI, both swapping occupation several times. There is an infomation panel outside.

From Hill 60 travel north to Ieper following signs.

(13) Ieper (Ypres)
Parking: N50°50.848' E002°52.610' around train station.

Ypres was known as Wipers by British soldiers during the war. The town was strategically important and was fought over throughout the war. It is believed that Ieper was the first place chemical weapons were used. In addition, the Battle of Passchendaele was fought here in 1917. A town map is located on pages 20-21.

(L) The Menin Gate
N50°51.121' E002°53.468'
Free entry; Open daily. Last Post 8pm daily. www.lastpost.be

The Menin Gate Memorial is located on the east side of town where soldiers departed to the battlefield. The memorial commemorates British soldiers who died in the area up to 1917 but have no known grave.

The Last Post is sounded at Menin Gate every day at 8pm. To show respect spectators are asked to remain quiet and not to applaud during or after the ceremony.

(M) In Flanders Fields Museum
N50°51.058' E002°53.128'
Adults €9; Compulsory refundable bracelet €1; Bell tower €2. Open Apr-Nov 10am-6pm; Nov-Mar Tue-Sun 10am-5pm. www.inflandersfields.be

Museum in Ieper dedicated to west Flanders during WWI.

From here travel to either Bruges, see page 43 for the linear route, or Bastogne, see page 22 for the circular route.

Ieper (Ypres)
www.toerismeieper.be

Park
P Stationstraat
N50°50.848' E002°52.610'

Eat
✕ In Ieper (Ypres), there are several restaurants around the market square.

✕ In't Klein Stadhuis   €-€€
N50°51.094' E002°53.168'
Grote Markt 32
www.inhetkleinstadhuis.be

Shop
🏛 Ieper has three main shopping streets: Menestraat, Rijselstraat and Boterstraat. There is also a market in the Market Square on Saturday mornings.

Stay
🅰 Jeugdstadion Ieper   €€
N50°50.814' E002°53.885'
Bolwerkstraat 122
www.jeugdstadion.be
Campsite open Mar-Nov
Motorhome parking all year

🏛 Albion Hotel   €€€
N50°50.980' E002°53.386'
Sint-Jacobsstraat 28
www.albionhotel.be

Further information
☑ "WWI's Tunnels of Death: The Big Dig" A two-part programme detailing a 2012 archaeological dig at Mesen. Filmed by Channel 5. www.channel5.com/shows/ww1s-tunnels-of-death-the-big-dig

☑ *Beneath Hill 60* 2010 feature film about the Australian miners tunnelling under the Messines ridge.

☑ For more WWI history and sites visit www.greatwarcentenary.be

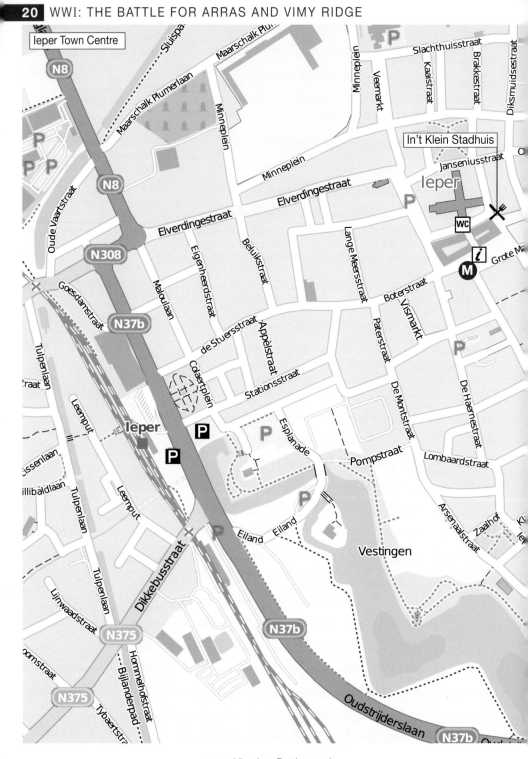

Ieper Town Centre

In't Klein Stadhuis

Ieper

Vestingen

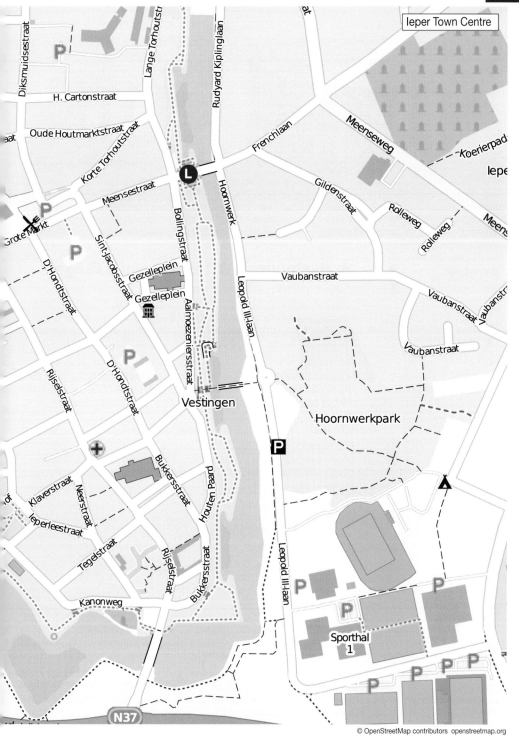

Ieper Town Centre

Mardasson Memorial, Bastogne.

Bastogne

www.paysdebastogne.be

Park

P Avenue Albert Ier   ✗
N49°59.918' E005°42.923'

Eat

✗ Brasserie Lamborelle   €
N50°00.129' E005°42.956'
Rue Lamborelle 19
www.brasserielamborelle.be
Beer bar and restaurant. Try the
Airbourne speciality beer.

✗ Le Nut's   €
N50°00.063' E005°42.935'
Place McAuliffe

Shop

▥ Along Rue du Sablon there
are lots of shops and
restaurants to choose from.

Stay

🚐 Bastogne Stopover   ✗
N49°59.907' E005°42.885'
Rue d'Assenois
20; Serviced

⛺ Camping de Renval   €€
N50°00.190' E005°41.726'
Rue de Marche 148
Open all year
www.campingderenval.be

★ Bastogne: WWII Battle of the Bulge

Parking: N49°59.907' E005°42.885'

> *Enter Bastogne on the N84 from the east. At the roundabout go straight over, sp 'Centre'. In 150m turn left into the car park, sp 'P Gratuit'.*

Six months after the WWII Normandy beach landings American and Allied troops reached the German border. On the 16th of December 1944 the Nazis launched the Ardennes counter offensive. The popular name for this is the Battle of the Bulge. American troops were forced back to Bastogne and by the 21st of December they had been surrounded. The next day the Nazi command requested that General McAuliffe surrender Bastogne. He replied: 'NUTS!' This was lost in translation, but clarification was given: 'Go to hell'. McAuliffe's troops held out until the 26th of December when they were saved by General Patton's 4th Armoured Division. Intense fighting continued into January, but the Nazi offensive lost momentum because of fuel shortages. On the 7th of January Hitler allowed his troops to withdraw. 19,000 American soldiers and 6,800 German soldiers were killed during the Battle of the Bulge.

> *🚶 In the corner of the car park visit General Patton's memorial and read the information panel about Patton. From here you can follow a succession of information panels around the town.*

(14) The town square is 250m from the car park, see city map on pages 24-25. The first thing you will see, if it is not camouflaged by tourists, is a Sherman tank. A bust of General McAuliffe stands on a plinth next to the Sherman and the Tourist Office.

> *From Bastogne drive, walk or cycle to the **Mardasson Memorial (15)**, which is well signed from the town. There are tank turrets alongside the road. Free parking outside the memorial.*

Above Mardasson Memorial, Bastogne. **Above right** General Patton's memorial. **Right** American tank.

Bastogne and surroundings

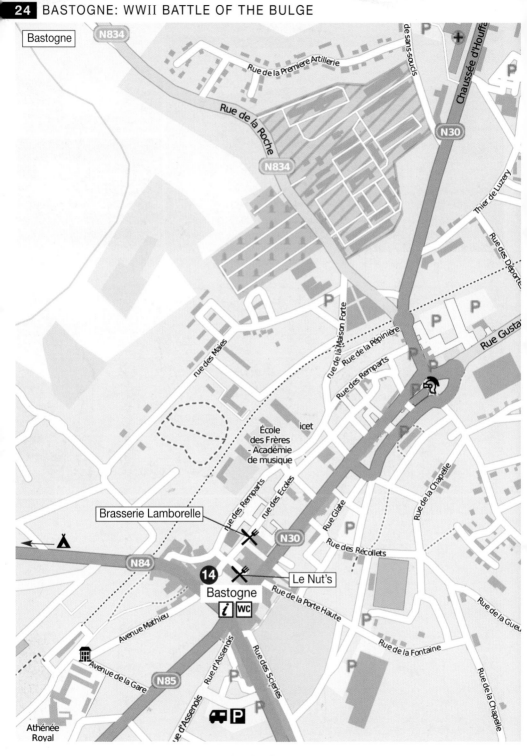

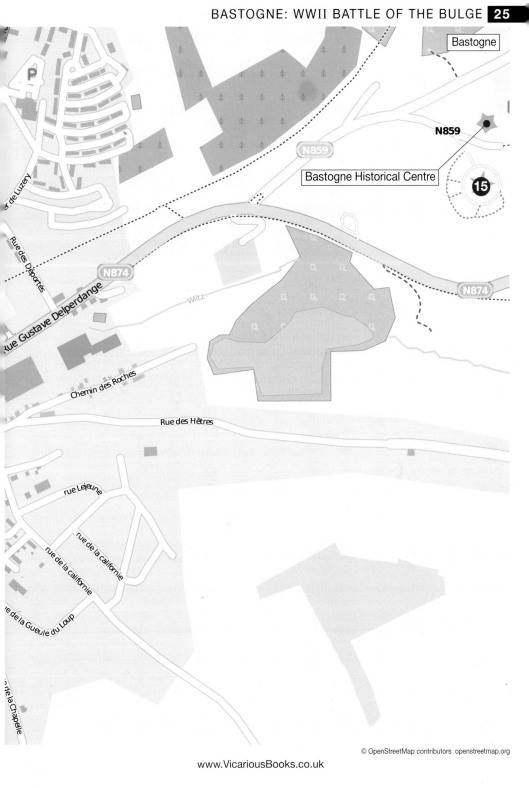

Bastogne

N859

Bastogne Historical Centre

15

Rue de Luzey

Rue des Déportés

N859

N874

Rue Gustave Delperdange

Wiltz

N874

Chemin des Roches

Rue des Hêtres

rue Lejeune

rue de la californie

rue de la californie

ue de la Gueule du Loup

le la Chapelle

© OpenStreetMap contributors openstreetmap.org

Top left and left Marshall Monument, Bastogne. **Right** Parking in Bastogne.

🏛 Best Western Hotel Melba €€
N49°59.988' E005°42.638'
49 Avenue Mathieu
www.melbahotel.com

Additional places to visit

🔫 Bastogne Historical Centre
N50°00.636' E005°44.349'
Adults €12, Children €8; Open
Mon-Fri 10am-5pm, Sat-Sun
and public and school holidays
10am-6.30pm.
Exhibit includes a 30-minute
video of the battle in English.
www.bastognewarmuseum.be

Further information

ℹ️ Tourist Office in town
square. Open daily 9.30am-
5.30pm.
www.paysdebastogne.be

ℹ️ Information on American
cemeteries and memorials from
the American Battle
Monuments Commission, see
www.abmc.gov

(15) Mardasson Memorial
N50°00.713' E005°44.387'
Free entry; Open daily.

The memorial is shaped as a five-pointed star and the battle history is engraved inside the star. The memorial commemorates the 76,890 American soldiers that were missing, wounded or killed during the Battle of the Bulge. There are additional maps on the information panel as well as signposted walks and cycle routes from here. Walk up the spiral steps for vistas over the battleground.

> *From Bastogne follow sp 'Recogne' onto the N30. After 4.5km turn left at the traffic lights, sp 'Recogne'. The **Recogne Cemetery (16)** is on the left in 800m. There is parking outside the cemetery.*

(16) Recogne German Cemetery
N50°02.962' E005°44.472'
Free entry; Open daily.

More than 6,800 German soldiers who were killed in the area rest in this cemetery. Originally the cemetery contained American and German dead, but in 1947 the American soldiers were either repatriated to the United States or reburied at **Henri-Chapelle American Military Cemetery** 96km to the north, N50°41.785' E005°53.931', **Neuville-en-Condroz American Military Cemetery**, 82km north, N50°32.503' E005°28.156', or at the **Luxembourg American Military Cemetery**, see below.

> *Drive through Luxembourg to the **Luxembourg American Military Cemetery (17)**, to the east of Luxembourg city. Exit the A1 at Junction 7 and follow signs to 'Sandweiler'. Turn first right and in 100m turn into the car park on the right. Fuel is cheaper in Luxembourg than neighbouring countries and appears to be price fixed.*

(17) Luxembourg American Military Cemetery
N49°36.786' E006°11.239'
Free entry; Open daily.

This 50-acre cemetery contains some of the troops who were killed or fought in the Battle of the Bulge, including General George S. Patton. There is a visitor centre in the entrance. Maps detail the battles fought throughout the area including the Battle of the Bulge.

Near the entrance there is a white stone chapel set on a circular platform. On either side of the chapel are stone pylons inscribed with the names of 371 missing troops. Rosettes beside the names identify the bodies that have since been recovered.

General Patton's grave is at the front of the cemetery between two flag poles. He actually died in a car accident after the war but requested to be buried with his troops.

> From here travel to Trier. Take the A1 out of Luxembourg onto the 64 in Germany. Exit onto the 51 and follow sp 'Trier'.

© OpenStreetMap contributors openstreetmap.org

Top left Ediger Eller Stellplatz. **Left** St Martinus Keller Ediger Burg, Moselle. **Right** The Moselle Valley.

The Moselle Valley
Trier
www.trier-info.de

Park

🅿 Messepark P+R
N49°44.334' E006°37.417'
In den Moselauen
See walking directions from
Treviris to town on page 30.
Bus 3 goes to the centre.

Eat

✗ Weingut Georg Fritz von
Nell   €
N49°44.328' E006°39.515'
Im Tiergarten 12, 2km from
centre.
www.vonnell.de
Try the wine soup!

✗ Restaurant Kartoffelkiste   €
N49°45.211' E006°38.334'
Fahrstraße 13
www.kiste-trier.de
Specialist potato restaurant.

Shop

🏬 Trier has four main
shopping streets:
Simeonstraße, Brotstraße,
Fleischstraße and Nagelstraße
These are flanked by side
streets which house more
shops to discover.

★ The Moselle Valley

The German Moselle River snakes through a beautiful, vine clad valley from Trier to Koblenz. Driving the valley road is a delight at all times of year. There are lovely walking and cycling trails along the Moselle River, where you can see fascinating historical ruins and museums. Trier sits on the banks of the Moselle and considers itself to be Germany's oldest town.

(18) Trier
Parking: N49°44.334' E006°37.417'
Start your Moselle tour in Trier. Trier has a wealth of Roman history because it was one of the capitals of the Roman Empire. The walk below takes in the key Roman ruins. There is a city map on pages 32-33.

🚶 *Roman Ruins and Marx*
Total distance: 3km, 1.8 miles.
From the Baths (N), walk into the gardens behind which make a good place for a picnic or a few quiet minutes. The next two points of interest are off these gardens. Exit the gardens to the right and visit the Rheinisches Landesmuseum (O) archaeological museum. Return to the gardens and exit at the far end at the Basilica (P). Cross the road and either walk along Liebfrauenstraße to the cathedral or down Palaststraße to Hauptmarkt, the main square: N49°45.402' E006°38.464'. From the main square exit into Simeonstraße. Stop outside the Tourist Office and the Porta Nigra (Q) city gate. Retrace your steps back to the main square. Exit the square into Fleischstraße, where you can browse the shops and visit the restaurants. Follow Fleischstraße into Karl-Marx Straße to the Karl Marx Haus museum (R). Continuing down Karl Marx Straße takes you back to the river where you can cross the bridge and turn left to follow the river back to your vehicle.

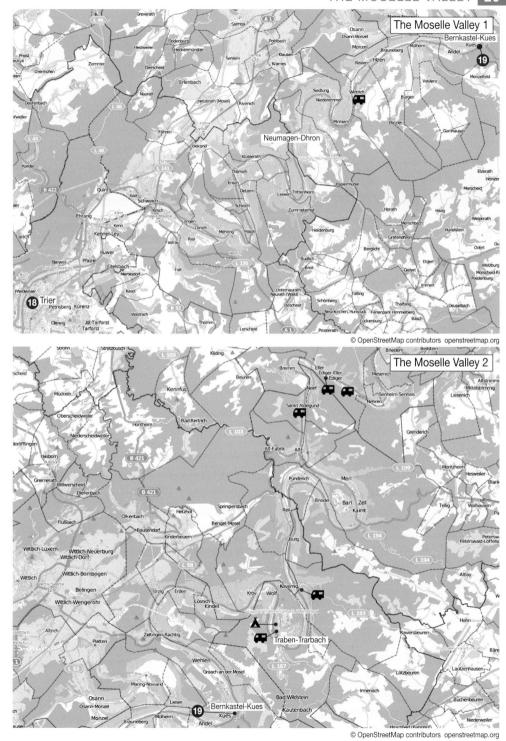

The Moselle Valley 1

The Moselle Valley 2

© OpenStreetMap contributors openstreetmap.org

© OpenStreetMap contributors openstreetmap.org

Top left Karl Marx Museum, Trier. **Left** Trier Basilica. **Right** Moselle River cruise from Trier.

Stay

🚐 Reisemobilpark Treviris €
N49°44.420' E006°37.469'
130 spaces; Entrance is via
credit card operated barrier
Open all year

🏕 Campingplatz Treviris €
N49°44.680' E006°37.491'
120 spaces
Open all year
www.camping-treviris.de

🚶 From Treviris to Trier
centre: Walk along the river
path to the left. In 1km cross
the first river bridge. After
crossing the river turn right,
then first left into Kaiserstraße
and follow for 900m. Turn left
into Weberbach when you
see the ruins, then first right
to the Roman bath ruins.

🚐 Weingut Georg Fritz von Nell €
N49°44.328' E006°39.515'
15 spaces; Wed-Sat; inc low
amp elec and water
Please telephone 065 13 23 97
in advance and report to the
restaurant between 5-6pm

🚶 From Weingut von Nell to
Trier centre: Walk back to the
main road, then turn left and
follow the road for 1km. Past
the amphitheatre turn right.
Cross the railway track bridge
and you are opp **(N)**.

(N) Kaiserthermen Roman Baths
N49°45.036' E006°38.464'
Adults €3, children up to 17 €1.50; Open daily Apr-Sept 9am-6pm,
Oct and Mar 9am-5pm, Nov-Feb 9am-4pm. Last admittance 30 minutes
before closing.

The Kaiserthermen Roman Baths were commissioned at the beginning
of the 4th century AD by Constantine I. These were the largest baths
built outside of Rome. A great deal of the baths remain intact above and
below ground making this an inside/outside exhibit.

(O) Rheinisches Landesmuseum
N49°45.075' E006°38.660'
Adults €6, children up to 18 €3, group and family discounts available;
Open Tues-Sun 10am-5pm. www.landesmuseum-trier.de

This museum is full of archaeological finds. Of special interest are the
Roman gravestones and the largest preserved hoard of Roman gold in
the world. There is a free audio tour with information in English.

(P) Trier Basilica
N49°45.229' E006°38.588'
Free entry; Open Apr-Oct 10am-6pm daily. Nov-Mar 11am-noon and
3pm-4pm, Mon closed, Sun noon-1pm.

The basilica is the largest single room structure that has survived from
the Roman era. It is also known as the Roman Imperial throne room. It
is the oldest protestant church in Trier.

(Q) Porta Nigra
N49°45.574' E006°38.632'

Adults €3, children up to 17 €1.50, group and family discounts available;
Open daily Apr-Sept 9am-6pm, Oct and Mar 9am-5pm and Nov-Feb
9am-4pm. Last admission 30 minutes before closing. Dramatic tours
available in summer. There are 130 steps inside. Pay at the Tourist Office.

Bernkastel-Kues, Moselle.

The Porta Nigra is the oldest Roman gate and the most famous Roman building in Germany, and is a designated World Heritage site. This city gate is called the Porta Nigra (black gate) which harks back to medieval times and the black patina on the sandstone. The city wall was built in the 2nd century and the black gate is the only survivor of five gates. The gate became a church during the 11th century, if you look up inside the gate there are two grave inscriptions clearly visible on the first floor.

Opposite the Porta Nigra is a pink building with €uroland underneath, this is the house where Karl Marx lived until the age of 18.

(R) Karl Marx Haus
N49°45.231' E006°38.138'
Adults €4, student, family and group discounts available; Open daily mid Mar-Oct 10am-6pm and 10am-8pm on the first Fri of the month, Nov-mid Mar Mon 2pm-5pm and Tue-Sun 11am-5pm.

The Karl Marx museum is housed within the house that Karl Marx was born in and lived in until he was 18 months old. He then lived above €uroLand as above. There are few artefacts within the museum but there are plenty of information panels.

> *From Trier follow the Moselle to Bernkastel-Kues.*

(19) Bernkastel-Kues
Parking: N49°55.106' E007°04.415'

The pleasant little town of Bernkastel is located on the opposite side of the Moselle River to its brother Kues. Bernkastel is packed full of quaint timber framed buildings that can be discovered via narrow streets. Climbing up the hill behind and north of Bernkastel is the Dr Loosen winery well known for Eiswein and Riesling.

🏨 Hotel Ante Porta   €€
N49°45.769' E006°38.923'
Paulinstrasse 66
www.hotel-anteporta.de

Tips and Tricks
☆ If you intend to visit all three Roman buildings on the listed walk it may be economical to purchase an Antiquity Card.

☆ Before you depart any attraction or café make sure you use the toilets as all public toilets charge €0.50pp.

☆ All the shops are closed on Sunday, but the restaurants are open.

Bernkastel-Kues
www.bernkastel.de

Park
🅿 Bernkastel   €
N49°55.106' E007°04.415'

🚐 Kues   €
N49°54.690' E007°04.065'
Follow the motorhome signs
Day parking only: 10am-6pm

Eat
✕ Graacher Tor   €€
N49°54.973' E007°04.555'
Graacher Straße 3
www.graacher-tor.com

✕ Alte Kanzlei   €
N49°55.031' E007°04.472'
Gestade 3, opp parking
www.altekanzlei-bks.de

Shop
🏪 On the Bernkastel side of the river there is the Markt which is full of shops and boutiques large and small.

Stay
🛖 Camping Kueser Werth   €€
N49°54.610' E007°03.180'
Am Hafen 2, Kues
www.camping-kueser-werth.de
Open April-Oct

🚐 Sun-Park Wohnmobilepark Graach   €€
N49°56.106' E007°03.667'
Gestade 16, Graah
www.sunpark-mosel.de
Open Mar-Oct

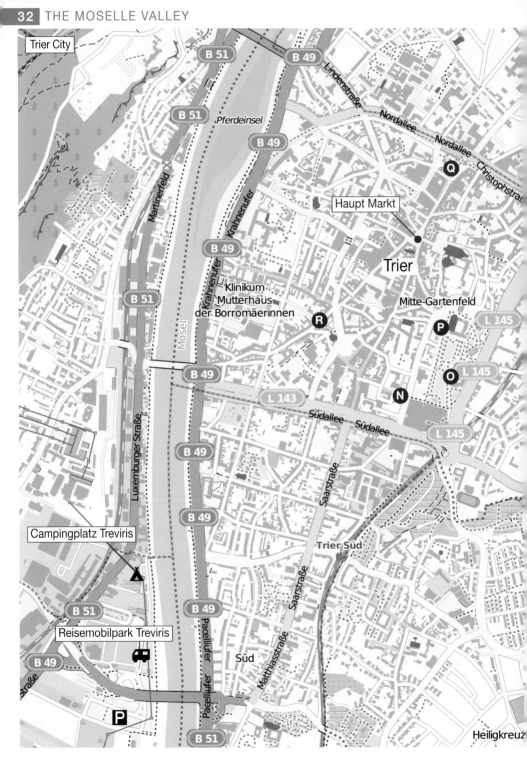

Trier City

B 51

B 49

Lindenstraße

Nordallee

Nordallee

Christophstraße

B 51

Pferdeinsel

B 49

Martinerfeld

Krahnenufer

Q

Haupt Markt

Trier

B 49

Krahnenufer

Klinikum
Mutterhaus
der Borromäerinnen

Mosel

Mitte-Gartenfeld

L 145

R

P

B 51

B 49

O

L 145

N

L 143

Südallee

Südallee

L 145

Luxemburger Straße

B 49

Saarstraße

Campingplatz Treviris

B 49

Trier Süd

B 51

B 49

Reisemobilpark Treviris

Saarstraße

Pacelliufer

Süd

Matthiasstraße

…Straße

P

Pacelliufer

B 51

Heiligkreuz

🏛 Christiana's WeinArt Hotel €€
N49°55.560' E007°03.682'
Lindenweg 18
www.wein-arthotel.de

The rest of Moselle

There are plenty of campsites,
motorhome stopovers, and
hotels along the Moselle. A
selection is detailed below
(listed from nearest to Trier):

🚐 Wohnmobil Stellplatz
Wintrich   €
N49°53.002' E006°56.899'
Mosellestraße
www.moselstellplatz.de
Open April-Oct

⛺ Campingplatz Rissbach   €€
N49°57.683' E007°06.349'
95 pitches, a third of which are
riverside pitches overlooking
the Moselle
www.moselcampingplatz.de
Open April-Oct

🚐 Traben Trarbach Motorhome
Stellplatz   €
N49°57.819' E007°06.334'
45 spaces
Open Apr-Nov

🚐 Enkirch   €
N49°59.020' E007°07.266'
Inc electricity

🚐 St Aldegund   €
N50°04.738' E007°07.867'
Inc service and electricity

🚐 Ediger Eller   €
N50°05.959' E007°08.641'

🚐 Ediger   €
N50°05.601' E007°09.567'

Tips and Tricks

☆ Be careful parking adjacent
to the Moselle in the winter
because it floods. Police will
warn visitors/guests when
flooding is expected. If the
police ask you to move your
vehicle, move it!

☆ If you wish to enjoy wine
tasting it would be better to
cycle, walk or boat. See
www.kolb-mosel.de or your
nearest pontoon for river boat
timetables.

✗ In Ediger
Weinrestaurant St
Martinuskeller
N50°05.757' E007°09.386'
Serves large portions of good
food in a cellar.
www.martinuskeller.de

Festivals

🎭 The Moselle Music Festival
takes place along the moselle
river each year from July-Oct.
www.moselmusikfestival.de

🎭 There is a wine festival,
Weinfest der Mittelmoselle, the
first weekend in September.

🎭 Bernkastel-Kues Christmas
market starts on Dec 6. In the
market square a house with 24
windows becomes an advent
calendar with a calendar
window opened at 5:30pm
each day in Dec.

Further information

ℹ️ Tourist Office in Moselle-
Gäste-Zentrum. Open Apr-Oct
Mon-Fri 9am-5pm, Sat 10am-
5pm and Sun 10am-1pm.

ℹ️ More information about
Moselle wine can be found at
www.weinland-mosel.de

ℹ️ Adjacent to the Vinothek is
a wine museum where you can
learn about local wine
production.
www.moselweinmuseum.de

Vinotheque wine tasting in Bernkastel-Kues.

*On foot/cycle cross the river bridge from Bernkastel into Kues. Turn right at the roundabout and the **Vinothek (S)** is in 70m on the right.*

(S) Vinothek

N49°54.983' E007°04.221'

€15 tasting, plus €2 glass deposit; Open Mon-Sat Apr-Oct 10am-6pm, Feb-Mar, Nov-Dec 11am-5pm. www.moselweinmuseum.de

Wine connoisseurs may well think this is the best thing Bernkastel-Kues has to offer as there are up to 130 local wines to taste at your leisure. Pay €15 at the till, plus €2 deposit for a glass, and then descend into the cellar where you can read about the wines (in German). Each wine has a number, so to taste go to the chiller with the wine's number, remove the wine, pour and taste. If you want to buy the wine, place an unopened bottle in a basket and take it to the till upstairs when you leave.

A local wine called Römerhof (www.roemerwein.de) is produced by an Australian using a combination of techniques. It is slightly different to the other Moselle valley wines and is worth a taste.

For the circular route head north to Eifel National Park, see page 35.

If you are following the linear route you are now at the end of your tour. From here you can enjoy driving the length of the Moselle. There are plenty of quaint towns to visit and lots of places to stop.

Vogelsang, Eifel National Park.

★ Eifel National Park

We've all heard the myths about wild cats roaming the UK and Europe but what if one day you discovered it was true? At Eifel National Park you really could see one of the 50 wild cats known as the Little Eifel Tiger. These cats look like a large tabby cat with a white beard. To increase your chances of sighting one of these elusive creatures, follow the cat face markers through 110km² of wilderness, beech, and oak forests. You are sure to see some of the other 1,600 species of endangered animals and plants. There are so many marked walking, cycling and mountain biking trails through the park it is worth purchasing a copy of the map, Nationalpark-Karte 1:25000 Wanern, Radfahren, Reiten. Maps are available from the Vogelsang shop. There is a pleasant, hilly footpath from the nearby village of Morsbach to Vogelsang. Overall this is a very beautiful location and keen walkers and cyclists could easily spend a week in the area.

Within the Eifel National Park visit **Vogelsong (20), Hürtgenwald (21)** and **Simonskall (22).** These areas feature different elements of WWII, including a Nazi Officer training ground and a battle field.

> *Vogelsang is located on the 266 between the villages of Einruhr and Herhahn. It is possible to park at the gateway and walk 2km or pay for parking in the grounds.*

(20) Vogelsang

N50°34.096' E006°26.195'
Free entry; Parking €3; Open daily, 10am-5pm, Christmas Eve and New Year's Eve 10am-2pm. German language tours depart at 2pm daily and 11am on weekends and bank holidays, €5. www.vogelsang-ip.de

Eifel National Park
www.nationalpark-eifel.de

Eat

✕ Café Kern   €
N50°40.045' E006°21.267'
Simonskall
For light bites and coffee.
www.cafe-kern.de

✕ Zum Alten Forsthaus   €€
N50°41.139' E006°21.030'
Germeter 49 Hürtgenwald
www.zum-alten-forsthaus.de

✕ Mestrenger Mühle   €
N50°40.359' E006°23.163'
Vossenack
www.mestrenger-muehle.de

Stay

🚐 Hürtgenwald   ✗
N50°42.320' E006°21.612'
5 spaces; No services.
In the car park adj to the cemetery

🚐 Simonskall   ✗
N50°40.026' E006°21.255'
10 spaces; Max 3.5t;
No services
In the village car park
Simonskall is located off L160
en route to Hürtgenwald.

🚐 Wohnmobil am Nationalpark
Eifel   €€
N50°34.699' E006°29.551'
pfarrer-kneippstraße, Gemund
www.womo-nationalpark-eifel.eu

⛺ Heimbacher Campingplatz €€
N50°38.569' E006°28.481'
Heimbach
Open all year

🏛 Zum Alten Forsthaus   €€
N50°41.139' E006°21.030'
Germeter 49 Hürtgenwald
www.zum-alten-forsthaus.de

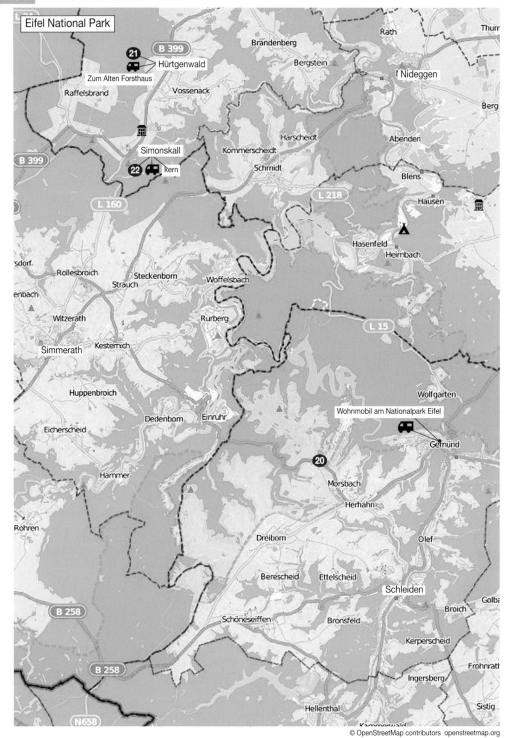

Eifel National Park

B 399

21 Hürtgenwald
Zum Alten Forsthaus

Raffelsbrand

Vossenack

Brandenberg

Bergstein

Rath

Thum

Nideggen

Berg

B 399

Simonskall

22 Kern

L 160

Harscheidt

Kommerscheidt

Schmidt

L 218

Abenden

Blens

Hausen

Hasenfeld

Heimbach

sdorf.

Rollesbroich

Steckenborn

Strauch

Woffelsbach

enbach

Witzerath

Kesternich

Rurberg

Simmerath

Huppenbroich

Dedenbom

Einruhr

Wolfgarten

Wohnmobil am Nationalpark Eifel

Gemünd

Eicherscheid

20

Morsbach

Hammer

Herhahn

Rohren

Dreibom

Olef

Berescheid

Ettelscheid

Schleiden

Golba

Broich

B 258

Schöneseiffen

Bronsfeld

Kerperscheid

Frohnrath

B 258

Ingersberg

Sistig

N658

Hellenthal

Above Hürtgenwald Cemetery. **Top right** Vogelsang Nazi camp. **Right** Parking in Hürtgenwald.

Vogelsang is an open access site consisting of numerous buildings used as an officer training camp by the Nazis. Vogelsang remained an army camp post war occupied by Belgian/NATO soldiers until 2008. The camp was so well designed that few changes were made. The buildings are arranged over a terraced hillside and occupy 100 hectares (247 acres or $1km^2$). Most of the buildings are closed, but there are windows for you to peer through.

Multilingual information panels detail the significance of each building or sculpture making it very easy to self-tour. The main building accommodates a café and shop that sells walking maps and has tourist information leaflets.

(21) Hürtgenwald
N50°42.320' E006°21.612'

> *Free parking outside Hürtgenwald, adj to the 399, at the open access German Military Cemetery.*

American and German troops fought fierce battles in the local area for six months during the winter of 1944 and 1945. The difficult terrain was underestimated by the advancing American commanders. Over 30,000 American and over 25,000 German casualties were recorded.

(22) Simonskall
N50°40.026' E006°21.255'

> *Turn off the 339, sp 'Simonskall'. Park in the village car park, 3.5t weight restricted.*

The 3.5t restricted car park is located in a small village which has a couple of restaurants. An information board provides details of a walk that passes several WWII bunkers. Alternatively you can make up your own walk using the clear walking signs and the map detailed in the Eifel National Park introduction on page 35. Numerous footpaths run through the village and across the surrounding valleys.

> *For the circular route head north to Valkenburg in the Netherlands, see page 38. If you are following the linear route head south to Bastogne in Belgium, see page 22.*

Top left Parking in Valkenburg. **Left** Valkenburg Christmas market. **Right** Wilhelmina Tower toboggan run and chairlift.

Valkenburg
www.vvvzuidlimburg.nl

Park
🅿 Burgemeester Henssinger €
N50°51.791' E005°50.213'

🚐 Burgemeester Henssinger €
N50°51.791' E005°50.213'

Eat
✗ The town centre has numerous cafés and restaurants.

✗ Aan de Linde €
N50°51.901' E005°49.879'
Jan Deckerstraat 1b
www.aandelinde.eu

✗ Le Fleur €€€
N50°51.831' E005°49.741'
Plenkertstraat 16
www.bijlafleur.nl

Shop
⚜ The pedestrianised town centre has Christmas shops and plenty of quaint streets to explore.

Stay
🚐 Valkenburg Stopover 2 €€€
N50°51.561' E005°49.886'
30 spaces; Max 48hrs
Custom

★ Valkenburg: Christmas year-round in the Dutch mountains

Parking: N50°51.791' E005°50.213'

Valkenburg sits at the foot of the Dutch mountains. Not actually mountains but at 100m above sea level they are the highest hills in Holland.

(23) Valkenburg Centre
Valkenburg is a popular tourist town all year around but especially leading up to Christmas. The towns building's are made from sandstone rock, excavated from under the town. The compact pedestrianised centre contains plenty of restaurants and shops, see city map on pages 40-41. The whole town dons festive decorations from mid-November to the end of December. Many of the shops are crammed with Christmas decorations and some sell Christmas all year around.

The caves under the town are open for escorted tours throughout the year and house Christmas Markets in December.

No mountain destination would be complete without a chairlift and some downhill action and Valkenburg has both: a 200m chairlift and a metal toboggan run. At the top of the chairlift is Wilhelmina Tower, a café and the entrance to the toboggan run. From the top of Wilhelmina Tower there are panoramic views of the local area including several wind and water mills and six castles.

(T) Wilhelmina Tower
N50°51.606' E005°50.050' (chairlift)
Chairlift: €4.50, €8.50 including 4 toboggan runs; Open daily 11am-5pm, but the chairlift may be closed some days in low season and the toboggan run is closed when it rains. Located on Neerhem Street. www.agogovalkenburg.nl

Valkenburg Christmas market in the caves.

The tower is 30m high and was built in 1906. On a crystal clear day you may be able to see Belgium and Germany.

ऀ *Towers, Caves and Castles*
Total distance: 1.8km, 1.1 miles
Start at the chairlift on Neerhem Street. Take the chairlift to the top and then climb **Wilhelmina Tower (T)** *and ride the toboggan. The tower and café can also be reached on foot by taking the stairs next to the Atlanta Hotel and following the path uphill for 250m. When you're ready, descend the hill on foot back to Neerhem Street. Turn left and follow Neerhem Street for 100m and then turn left again onto a stepped path alongside the castle walls. Visit* **the castle and its cave network (U).** *Exit the castle onto Daalhemerweg and turn right. Walk to the end of the street, passing Aarts Christmas World. If you wish to visit more caves or another Christmas market, turn left into Cauberg street and the entrance to the* **Gemeentegrot cave (V)** *is in 20m on the right. Alternatively turn right and in 20m pass through Grendelpoort gate into the pedestrian town. Explore the quaint streets, numerous cafés and restaurants and the Christmas shops.*

(U) The Velvet Cave and Castle Ruins
N50°51.673' E005°49.819'
€9 including access to the castle ruins; Open daily although the castle ruins may be closed in bad weather. The entrance is on Daalhmerweg, at a zebra crossing. www.fluweelengrot.nl

This cave (Fluweelengrot) was created due to marl extraction and is more than 10 miles long. Much of the marl taken from this cave was used for the construction of Valkenburg castle.

Throughout history the cave has served many purposes, including as an escape route from the castle when under siege. When Napoleon held the town captive an alter was carved into the rock in a large room which became a chapel for church services and baptisms. More recently the caves provided shelter for the citizens of Valkenburg during WWII.

The hilltop castle ruins date back to the 11th century. Information panels in English explain the castle's fraught history. As you walk from panel to panel you also take in wonderful views of the town and the valley spreading beyond.

Valkenburg City

Leenhoflaan

allandtlaan

Koningswinkelstr

Broekhem

Statenlaan

De Valkenier

Wiegert

Prinses Beatrixsinger

Prin.

Odapark

Geul

Geul

Geul

Polfermolen

Plenkertstraat

Plenkertstraat

Valkenburg

Cauberg

Cauberg

Valkenburg aan de Geul

Trichtergrube

Thermae 2000

Trichterberg aquariumgrot

Cauberg

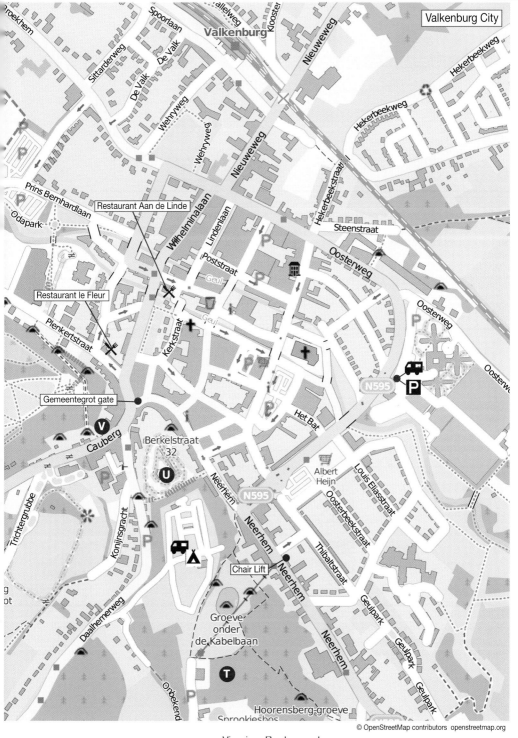

Valkenburg City

Valkenburg motorhome stopover and campsite.

🅰 Camping de Cauberg €€
N50°51.561' E005°49.886'
Open all year.
ACSI Camping Card accepted
www.campingdecauberg.nl

🏨 Hotel Scheepers €€
N50°51.916' E005°50.080'
Sint Pieterstraat 18
www.hotelscheepers.nl

Festivals

✂ Around mid November
Valkenburg opens as a
Christmas town with nativity
scenes, Christmas parades and
Christmas markets in the
Fluweelengrot and
Gemeentegrot caves.
www.kerststadvalkenburg.nl

Tips and Tricks

☆ When buying mulled wine
you first need to purchase a
cup, these usually have a
novelty design and cost a few
Euros. You then buy the mulled
wine which is placed in your
cup. Once you have finished
your drink you can either return
your cup for a refund or keep it
as a souvenir.

(V) Gemeentegrot Cave
N50°51.741' E005°49.755'

€6; Open daily, times vary throughout the year; An escorted tour takes 1
hour on foot or 30 mins by train. The cave entrance is on Cauberg street
which is near the base of the castle. www.gemeentegrot.nl

*For the circular route head west to Bruges in Belgium, see page 43.
If you are following the linear route, head east to the Eifel National
Park in Germany, see page 35.*

Gemeentegrot cave entrance during the Christmas market.

Above Minnewater Park, Bruges. **Right** Timmermans produce Lambic beer.

★ Bottoms Up in Bruges

Parking: N51°11.783' E003°13.510'

Bruges, a UNESCO World Heritage site, is very attractive and has a vibrant brasserie culture. Brasserie means brewery, and Bruges is an ideal place to enjoy a small but strong beer, and watch the world and many tourists go by. As is common at most top tourist spots there are plenty of tourist shops and activities.

(24) Bruges Centre
The small medieval centre oozes charm all year. There is a map on pages 44-45.

(W) De Halve Maan Brewery
N51°12.148' E003°13.456'
Brewery tours every hour, €7.50; Open daily Apr-Oct 11am-4pm, except Sat 11am-5pm, Nov-Mar Mon-Fri 11am-3pm and Sat-Sun 11am-4pm. www.halvemaan.be

This brewery was established in 1856 and it is the only family run brewery in Bruges centre that is still active. There is a restaurant/bar on site where you should try Brugse Zot, which is brewed on site.

(X) The Chocolate Line
N51°12.398' E003°13.345'
Open daily, Tue-Sat 9.30am-6.30pm, Sun-Mon 10.30am-6.30pm. www.thechocolateline.be

Unfortunately there is no such things as cheap Belgian chocolates, despite the numerous chocolate shops in Bruges. However, it's worth taking a look at the magnificent array of hand crafted yumminess. You can even live like the Rolling Stones and snort some chocolate with the chocolate shooter!

Bruges
www.visitbruges.be

Park

🅿 Buiten Katelijnevest   ✗
N51°11.783' E003°13.510'
Roadside parking

🚐 Bruges Stopover   €€€
N51°11.783' E003°13.510'

Eat
✗ There are hundreds of restaurants and cafés to choose from in Bruges.

✗ Books and Brunch   €
N51°12.265' E003°13.774'
Garenmarkt 30
www.booksandbrunch.be

✗ Park Restaurant + B+B   €€€
N51°12.439' E003°13.851
Minderbroedersstraat 1
www.parkrestaurant.be

✗ Beerbrasserie Cambrinus   €
N51°12.571' E003°13.569
Philipstockstraat 23
www.cambrinus.eu

Shop
🎪 Bruges' main high street shopping area is around Zuidzandstraat and Steenstraat, but the area surrounding its two market places is also brimming with shops and stalls selling a variety of products.

Bruges City

Ruddershove

Ruddershove

Ruddershove

N371

Sint-Pietersk
Sint-Pieterse
Sint-Pieters-O

Sint-Pieterskaai

Rustenburgstraat

Wijnenburgstraat

Kolenkaai
Kolenkaai

Leopold II-laan

Kanaal Gent-Brugge

Waggelwater

Steenkaai
Steenkaai

Houtkaai

Sport
Nautique
Brugge

N9

Kardinaal Mercierstraat

Werfstraat

Waggelwater

Kroonstraat

Sint-Lodewijkscollege

Karel de Floustraat

Leopold I-laan

Gouden Boomstraat

R30

Klaverstraat

N31

VTI Deeltijds
onderwijs

Karel de Stoutelaan

Kristus-Koning

Lauwerstraat

Filips de Goedelaan

Gulden Vlieslaan

Ezelstraat

Bevrijdingslaan

Waggelwater
(Zone
03)

Maria Van Bourgondiëlaan

Karel de Stoutelaan

Rozendal

N31

Bevrijdingslaan

N351

Fosterpark

Bevrijdingslaan

R30

Oude Zak

Beenhouwersstraat

Expressweg

Dirk Martensstraat

Pieter de Conincklaan

Peter Benoitlaan

Lange Vesting

Buiten Smedenvest

Guido Gezellelaan

Moerstraat

Dirk Martensstraat

Peter Benoitlaan

Sint Jansdreef

Sint-Andries

Lane Paalstraat

Noord

Hoge Lane Brugge-Oostende

Jan Breydellaan

Hogeweg

Vier Uitersten

Metronoom

Zwijnstraat

Legeweg

Hogeweg

10 Geboden

Legeweg

Hendrik Conscienceaan

R30

Legeweg

Noordveldstraat

Legeweg

't Zand

VTI Brugge

Hogeweg

Korte Vesting

Singel

VTI Brugge

C.I.B "De
Refuge"

Zandstraat

Stationslaan

Refugestraat

Zandstraat

N367

N32

Magdalenastraat

N397

Gistelse Steenweg

Sint-Baafsstraat

Stationslaan

steenweg

N367

Manitobalaan

Torhoutse Steenweg

Ontmijnersllaan

Brugge

Burggraaf de Nieulantlaan

Eigen Heerdlaan

Abdijbekestraat

Azalealaan

tje

Robrecht van Vlaandere

Riethuisstraat

Expressweg

A. Wybolaan

N31

Heerdlaan

Heenweg

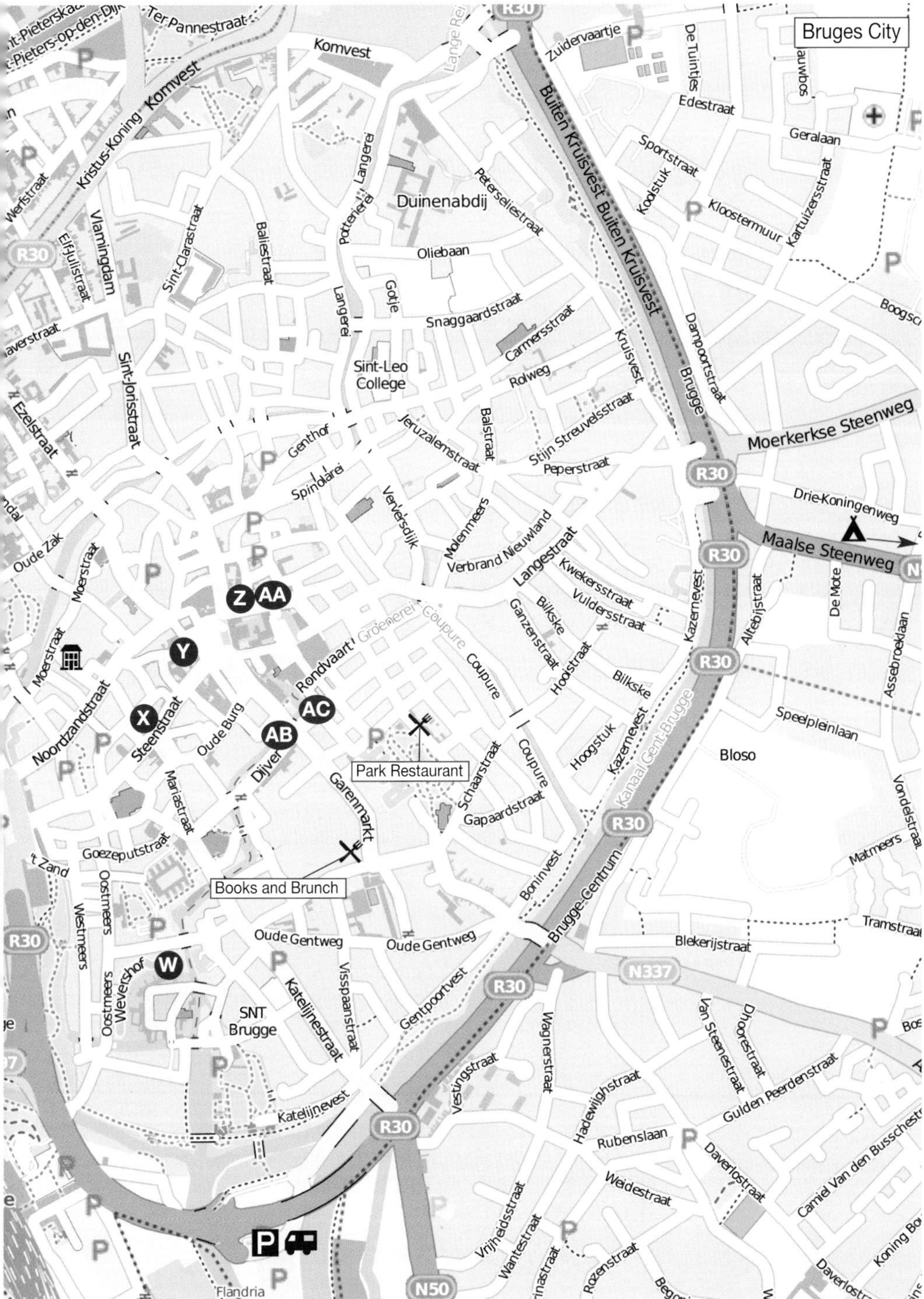

Bruges City
Park Restaurant
Books and Brunch
Z
AA
Y
X
AB
AC
W
Ter Pannestraat
Komvest
Kristus-Koning
Komvest
Lange Rei
Langerei
Potterierei
Duinenabdij
Peterseliestraat
Oliebaan
Gotje
Snaggaardstraat
Sint-Leo College
Carmersstraat
Rolweg
Balstraat
Jeruzalemstraat
Stijn Streuvelsstraat
Peperstraat
Genthof
Spinolarei
Verversdijk
Molenmeers
Verbrand Nieuwland
Langestraat
Kwekersstraat
Vuldersstraat
Bilkske
Ganzenstraat
Hooistraat
Rondvaart
Groenerei
Coupure
Hoogstuk
Kazernevest
Schaarstraat
Gapaardstraat
Boninvest
Garenmarkt
Dijver
Oude Burg
Mariastraat
Steenstraat
Noordzandstraat
Moerstraat
Oude Zak
Ezelstraat
Sint-Jorisstraat
Sint-Clarastraat
Baliestraat
Vlamingdam
Elfjulistraat
Werfstraat
Goezeputstraat
't Zand
Oostmeers
Westmeers
Wevershof
SNT Brugge
Oude Gentweg
Katelijnestraat
Visspaanstraat
Gentpoortvest
Katelijnevest
Flandria
Zuidervaartje
De Tuintjes
Edestraat
Geralaan
Sportstraat
Koolstuk
Kloostermuur
Kartuizersstraat
Buiten Kruisvest
Kruisvest
Dampoortstraat
Brugge
Moerkerkse Steenweg
Drie-Koningenweg
Maalse Steenweg
Altebijstraat
De Mote
Assebroeklaan
Speelpleinlaan
Bloso
Vondelstraat
Matmeers
Tramstraat
Blekerijstraat
Kanaal Gent-Brugge
Brugge-Centrum
Van Steenestraat
Dhoorestraat
Gulden Peerdenstraat
Wagnerstraat
Vestingstraat
Hadewijchstraat
Rubenslaan
Daverlostraat
Weidestraat
Camiel Van den Busschestraat
Vrijheidsstraat
Wantestraat
Rozenstraat
Begoniastraat
R30
N337
N50

Main Square, Bruges.

Stay

🚐 Bruges Stopover €€€€
N51°11.783' E003°13.510'
40 spaces; Serviced
Day parking opposite

⛺ Camping Memling €€
N51°12.438' E003°15.789'
Veltemweg 109
www.brugescamping.be
Open all year

🏨 Hotel Prinsenhof €€€€
N51°12.492' E003°13.176'
Ontvangersstraat 9
www.prinsenhof.com

Festivals

🎭 From mid Nov-Dec Bruges goes festive with a Christmas market, an outdoor ice rink in the market place, a snow and ice sculpture festival and lots of fairy lights.

🎭 The Bruges Beer Festival is in February and brings together more than 70 brewers and nearly 300 beers!
www.brugsbierfestival.be

🚶 *Beer and Chocolate in Bruges*
Total distance: 4km, 2.5 miles.
From the parking area walk/cycle under the flyover and follow the road round to the left. Turn right by the bus stop and walk into the park and cross a river bridge. Walk straight on through the park keeping Minnewater Lake on the left. This scenic park is a good place for a picnic. Carry on up a cobbled street keeping the river on your left. Turn left at the crossroads into Walplein and De Halve Maan Brewery (W) is 50m on the right. After the brewery turn right into Walstraat and then turn left at the end of the road into Kaltelijnestraat. In 300m fork right after the church into Mariastraat. Continue along Mariastraat for 160m to a pleasant square, and then continue straight on along the edge of the square to The Chocolate Line (X), a renowned chocolate shop. After The Chocolate Line turn right into Steenetraat and follow this road for 200m to the main market square (Y). With your back to the belfry exit the square at the right-hand corner into Philipstockstraat. If you want to pay homage to malt and hops visit the De Bier Tempel (Z) bottle shop, on the left. If all that choice has made you dry call into Beerbrasserie Cambrinus (AA), 70m further along the road. This famous restaurant and bar stocks 400 bottled beers and has around 10 beers on tap. Return to the main square and this time exit to the left of the belfry into Wollestraat. Follow the road to the river bridge where you can enjoy a leisurely river cruise (AB) or more beer at 2be (AC). After crossing the river bridge turn right and follow the road to the end. Turn left into Mariastraat and follow the road for 700m. Turn right before road crosses river. Follow the footpath alongside the river for 350m passing under the flyover and you have made it back to the car park.

Above Enjoy a beer in the main square, Bruges. **Right** The Belfry, Bruges.

(Y) Market Square and Belfry
N51°12.525' E003°13.461'

Belfry: €8; Open daily 9.30am-5pm. Restricted to 70 visitors at a time and can be busy, so visit early in the day.

To visit the top of the belfry you have to climb 366 steps, as you ascend you may recall the fight scene in the film 'In Bruges'. When you come back down to earth you can refresh yourself at one of the many cafés.

The square hosts a Christmas market during December and there is a food market on Wednesdays 8am-1pm throughout the year.

(Z) De Bier Tempel
N51°12.564' E003°13.516'
Open daily 9.30am-6.30pm. www.biertempel.be

This small shop stocks more than 600 different bottled beers and the accompanying glasses. Belgian beer is normally served in glasses designed especially for each individual beer. Breweries make a great effort not only to make superb beer but also to create eye catching designed and shaped glasses which make great souvenirs.

(AA) Beerbrasserie Cambrinus
N51°12.571' E003°13.569'
Open daily 11am-11pm, Sat-Sun until midnight. www.cambrinus.eu

Cambrinus is known as the King of Beer in several European countries and he is accredited with inventing beer. The building that houses Beerbrasserie Cambrinus dates to 1699 and has been a tavern at least since 1887. If you like good beer accompanied with good value food you may be here some time.

Tips and Tricks

☆ The Bruges City Card will give you discounts across a range of attractions like museums, the De Halve Maan brewery, bicycle hire and concerts and theatre as well as a free roundtrip canal ride (Mar-mid Nov). www.bruggecitycard.be

☆ Belgian beer is very strong and the Belgians have excellent snacks which ideally complement beer – and stop it going straight to your head. Order the assorted cold snacks, koude hapjes, which consists of paté, sausage or ham and cheese similar to Edam. At some brassieres it is possible to buy these items individually, for €2-€4 each, or combined on one platter.

Top left Parking in Bruges. **Left** Inner courtyard of the Belfry, Bruges. **Right** Cold snacks eaten with beer.

☆ When drinking beer it is advisable to start with the weakest beer and move up in strength, so you can taste the beers fully. At Cambrinus the beer menu can be a little overwhelming, try the Cambrivinus huisbier (house beer) both in blond and bruin with the assortiment koude hapjes (assortment of cold snacks) for €9. Staff speak English and menus are multilingual.

☆ If you wish to develop your beer knowledge further try Timmerman's Framboise (Raspberry) and Strawberry Lambic beers.

(AB) River Cruise
N51°12.426' E003°13.611'

€8; Open daily Mar-Nov 10am-6pm; Free with Bruges City Card. Trip lasts 30 minutes and there are five embarkation points in the town. www.visitbruges.be.

(AC) 2be
N51°12.435' E003°13.602'

Open daily 9.30am-7.30pm. www.2-be.biz

Opposite the river boats a wall of bottled beer is displayed by 2be. Once inside you can visit the shop, cellar and try numerous beers at the bar.

> *For the linear route head east to Valkenburg in the Netherlands, see page 38. If you are following the circular route you are now at the end of your tour. Calais is 115km (1hour 14mins).*

River Cruise.